The Lost Grip

The Lost Grip
Eva Zimet

Rootstock Publishing

The Lost Grip
©2020 Eva Zimet

All rights reserved.

No part of this book may be used or reproduced in any manner without written permission of the author, except in the case of brief quotations in critical articles or reviews.

For reprint information or to schedule an author reading,
please contact the author at eva.zimet@gmail.com.

Published by
Rootstock Publishing Poetry Series
Montpelier, Vermont
www.rootstockpublishing.com

Editor: Samantha Kolber

Book design by ENC Graphic Services
Artwork by Eva Zimet

Library of Congress Control Number: 2020915443
ISBN-13: 978-1-57869-042-8
Ebook ISBN-13 978-1-57869-043-5

Printed in the USA.

Acknowledgments

Thanks to Rachel Zimet for the contribution to the cover design, and thanks to the following places where some poems were previously published:

Montpelier ArtWalk 2020: "Haiku, More Likely Than Not"
Montpelier PoemCity 2017: "The Art"
Montpelier PoemCity 2019: "The Listening Book"
Montpelier PoemCity 2020 and Waterbury PoemWalk 2020: "Chime"

To my teachers.

grief is a thing I do

Record	1
Not Shown Here	2
The Lost Grip I	3
Escaping the Gaze	4
Tempo	5
Haiku, From ...	6
Disappeared / Desaparecido	7
Hold Me	8
Sense	9
So Close	10
Stars IRL	11
Trigger	12
I Call It My Lucky Star Scar	13
Roadkill	15
Home to Me	16
Chime	17
Risk	18
Tango	19
Haiku, More Likely ...	20

surviving trauma sometimes hurts

Those Who Can Say Chevre	23
1 Foot in The Door	24
Sense II	25
Haiku, Plot Twist	26
Do Not Follow	27
I'll Tell You Now	29
Tanka, If He ...	30
Odds	31
Raised Bed	32
Dreamspace for All of Us	33
The Listening Book	34
Grief Much?	35
Another Bat Poem	37
Not That Wake	38
I Know What I'm Looking For	39
A Lot	40
Slam	41
I Didn't See That Coming	42
Rebound	43
What Was It?	44
Blueprint ...	45

healing is a growth stock

I'm Not Done	49
Knowing You Then Is Saving Me Now	50
Every Little Fucking Thing Is a Masterpiece	51
You Asked and I Answered	52
La Tina	53
Snap	56
A Ripe Mango	57
The Lost Grip II	58
Sky, Open	59
The Fall	60
Thank You, I'm Sorry	61
Compás Beat	62
Sometimes I Like It Windy	63
Stay	64
Or Else, Or …	65
The Art	66
Hitch	67
Coincidentally	68
Trust	69
On *The Heart Sutra*	70
3 Jewels: A Commentary	71

Lift	72
Touch Me with Your Tactile Heart	73
App Quit, Rip	74

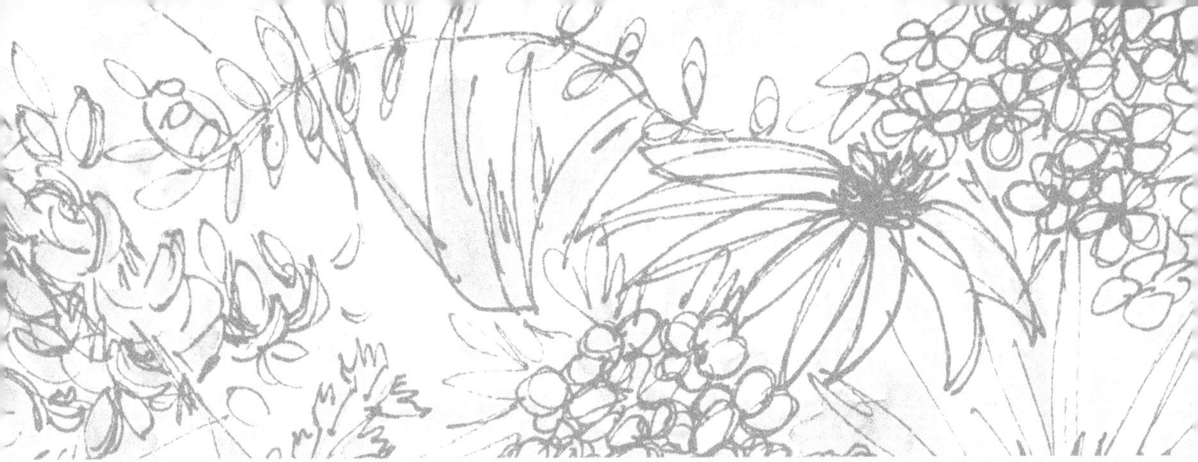

grief is a thing I do

Record

        Past the jamb
            I drop to the floor.
                The tears that flow
                    find the branch and
merge into the deep wide current where they are no longer sadness.
            The more I cry, the more I
                flood and carve
                      the stone bank
              into the
        necessary record.

NOT SHOWN HERE

The Lost Grip I

Don't, I won't catch every feeling
Like a scarce raindrop—
Bottle it up, call it some trendy, limbic, shit like that.
Pay to have it named and held against me.
I can let them spill.
Come more anyway.

Escaping the Gaze

I meet my eye by accident
                    A mirror is essentially a highly reflective surface
and startle.
                    allowing even subtle details to be clearly seen
I stop, lean in, look deep.
                    a very clean piece of glass sufficiently heated
My eyes are green and brown and blue.
                    the silver will precipitate
My hair curls in humid heat of summer.
                    part of the light will also be diffracted
Has this been me for long?

Tempo

Caches of rubble are the obstacles
      so slowly, geologically formed,
I took them as landmarks,
          orienting myself in accord.
But they shift under my feet at a tempo
        I fail to notice.

Haiku

From the point of view
of the dharma wheel turning,
everything's turning.

Disappeared

There was a morning moon.
I didn't get a picture,
but I got some words, here you have them, at least.
I'm glad — I looked again and the moon was gone.

Desaparecido

Había una luna de la mañana.
No tomé una foto,
pero algunas palabras, aquí las tienes al menos.
Me alegra — miré de nuevo y la luna ya no estaba allí.

Hold Me

The rasping breath
the spasmed chest
I don't need you.
I do.

Sense

Touch me in the language of your freed soul.
Make love to me like that.
I will understand you.

So Close

Your warmth rises to my surface.
In this way we touch, no matter the distance
because time is supple and space our dance.

Stars IRL

She can't see the stars, only me
and then darkness.
I tell her they are beautiful.

I see her. We can't touch and
I walk alone.

Trigger

A friend still a friend after time and again
before and while
it's all going
down

catches me by surprise and I'm hard put
not to have that frighten me
with the memory of loss.

I Call It My Lucky Star Scar

Flat leaf parsley trimmed,
pungent leaves bundled and stuffed into my mouth
chased with hard cheese, whiskey, and repeat
because this is dinner and I'm still hungry.

My neighbor grows the parsley and I'm in charge in her absence,
invited to harvest.
Where has she gone? She is not back yet.

I cut this bunch from her plot late day,
my room vibrates earth struck green
that pairs whiskey pleasantly, I think,
loosen my grip,
allow the past and now to mingle.

I walk up softly to and by the heaped-up thens,
splicing now onto
then left to die of a stomach wound
then burned in a careless fire
then pulled from the crash
then crawled up the stairs watched by the perpetrator of agony
from the top. *Look up to me,* said the gaze, and *why not just die?*

Then I survived.
Where have the others gone, though?

The bright taste of the parsley perfects the day,
the sunset rose shot flat leaf green.
Color blocks, felling clowns, calling out.

I fancy a status and all I got was this state, but it will do
more than enough. My simple self.
But where has my neighbor gone? Back soon?

Stripped with blunt violence I didn't invite
— you didn't think I did, did you —
scars made visible by surviving, by surviving I draw my scars
as talisman knots and revive my lot.

I gently store the memories one by one,
weaponize empathy, stock my armory
not for revenge, no.
With love.

In this way I fight
for my neighbor
in her absence.

Roadkill

I say a prayer for roadkill.
The prayer is Tibetan. I am not Tibetan.
But then again, I'm not the muskrat, either.
Or the fox, the groundhog or deer.
Not this time
around, so
I say a prayer wishing
the traveler a safe trip to the next place.
Anchors away, you know?
That's the gist.

Home to Me

In the middle of the day,
standing outside in the sun,
looking at the road,
I shift my glance to a car
coming by, and think
someone is coming home to me.
But no one is.

Chime

Church bells ring across town
2 chimes
It's early,
or very late.
The chimes ripple and roll in ten directions,
reaching me here.
The church does a good thing, ringing
the hour, and has met me, for the first time.
I chant and you chime, bells, you chime.

Risk

I asked to know you,
daring curiosity as a tangent to passion. I
wanted to share the freefall of intimacy
with you. Didn't happen.

Got the passion, *np* fucking is easy
although I did like how you did and didn't elaborate with our bodies.
You listened with yours and attended to mine. So good.
I wanted to know more of you. So daring?

Apparently.
Ghosted, returned, renewed and left
again when I dared again
to ask to know you.
Maybe you're laughing at me, now.
You might be satisfied that I do care and it does hurt.

Or maybe you're beset,
craving and missing the link.

Never mind.
I will take the risk again, but not with you.

Tango

Of what use am I?
Anyway, I planted those flowers.
They haven't sprouted yet, I know.
They know. Anyway,
you danced with me.
We laughed after the embrace that lit us up.

Haiku

More likely than not,
a rock will stay where it's put,
a person might choose.

surviving trauma sometimes hurts

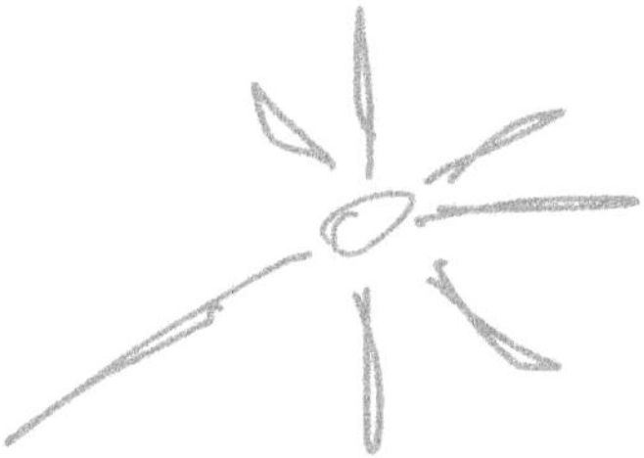

Those Who Can Say Chevre

Cardinals, the bright red paired with the red-grey.
Two blue jays fly by. Crows murder in groups.

With what would I pair well?
A fresh lemon & me?
Lavender garnish?
Real maple syrup.

Me: pairs well with others.
Also me: Delicious on my own. Pairs well with solitude.

1 Foot in the Door

I put 1 foot in the conversation
1 in my mouth
then quick outside
but *way* outside, space-outside,
can't-relate-to-the-inside outside
split in two, inside-out,
said the man in the hotel room
when I was young and he gave me
champagne to loosen me up.

or else just outside,
on-the-threshold outside
the way someone might say are you coming
or going?
and I'd like to think I know.

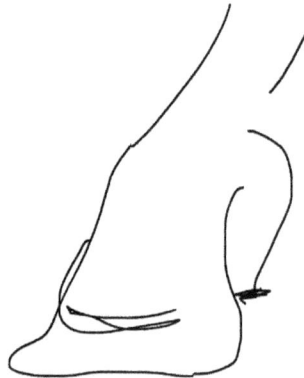

Sense II

My writhing soul is real.
You can't tell, I see.

When I catch your eye
it is a dense mesh, a tiny mask like the one you hung
on a nail in the wall with the loud story
I found was
female purification.
I took it down.

My writhing soul does not align with your sight picture.
Coiling now to strike.

Haiku, Plot Twist

The vine has tender
roots. If you clip them just right,
they will not grow back.

Do Not Follow

Little girl curled on the staircase,
me. I saw,
        wasn't meant to see
I heard
        wasn't meant to hear,
told not to tell, planting fear.

From these scraps I learn the pattern

now reformed now re-told.
I'm sorry the story is this old.

        eyes, nerves, clamps
        disappeared, sprung traps

My father broke but he'd already died.

Asked to do wrong he complied
because those who didn't were killed
or stilled
and he couldn't just say
he didn't want to obey.

I get it, he didn't want to die that way.

Not my path, not today.
The little girl grew
learned the slew of lies she heard
found the right word, alive.
Alive.

I'll Tell You Now

Through the end-of-life I washed and steadied him.
I managed his family visiting,
his coterie dismissing me.
He loved many men and women.
I held them back in the last days, for our children
to say goodbye.

I asked him to share his truth with me aloud, although I knew
his well-known secret.
He said people like me end up with a knife in their back.

Remarkably common, all of it.
The complicit silence, fear and pain.
The range of how we seek love and deny it.

Tanka

If he came alive
again now, I would not walk
toward him, I don't think
I would, leaving room for doubt,
and that could be a good thing.

•

Would he walk toward me?
I am at the gravesite now,
I brush off the leaves,
drag off the heavy windfall,
leaving the moss — he loved moss.

Odds

Flinty rock covers
the ground and against
the odds a green shoot.
Whose odds? Whose?

Raised Bed

I don't have your neat raised-bed gardens, my friend.
I got some old plastic bins. They will do. Punched holes
in them myself so the plants don't drown. Maybe
stacked two-high, those garbage tires will do
for next year, if we're here.

Dreamspace for All of Us

Ever since I met Daniel
and even before
I dreamed of a space for us,
any of us, all of us.
Before Daniel, I thought it was a church,
later a temple, a dojo, a studio.
Yeah, now a studio.
The floor is wide-planked and smooth.
The space is otherwise empty.
I sleep against the wall.
Daniel also slept by the wall in a studio, and he survived.
We are the most intimate, in that.

The Listening Book

I open a blank notebook
and find it full.

On one page, it tells me

Learning is a dangerous thing to do.

On another page I see that
Possibilities are endless – never give up.

Then,
I am not alone.
The frame must break, not me.

Next, a quiet page, listening.

It was listening all along.

Grief Much?

Fresh soil, deeper plot.
I did not kill myself but flailed. Instead,
I'm going to repot my soul.

Buried me grows in an earth womb
where I hide, alive, a seed in
fresh soil, deeper pot.

Those who have read the law, know
it would not be murder if he'd killed me.
I did replant my soul.

Stomach wounds are usually fatal,
says the doctor, leaving me on the table.
Fresh soil, deeper ground.

I can wait, I can wait, gestate,
while, ready-ready, relate,
kashered, my soul

finds the light and air.
Shoots of life.
Fresh soil, deeper land,
I revive my soul.

Another Bat Poem

What happens to a day?
Soft wind-slap like the bat at dusk.
We saw it. In the falling snow no less.
What happens to time?
Like the bat at dusk. Blending, still there, if gone from sight.
It's time we all share, know it or not.

Not That Wake

Blinking as if snapped
awake. I'm breathless
having survived the
night. Dreams, memories
of when she left me
there on the side of
the road. Dreams too of
how the blows fell. Not
yet able to see.
I'm writhing in its
aftershock as I
wake—wondering if
others are with me.

I Know What I'm Looking For

Marie-Karine frames blues mostly
from the changing sky and sews them
in round needlepoint frames.

When I want blue, I know blue,
the frequency, sensate.
There are many blues. We know this, Marie-Karine and I.
We might disagree on the shade, or how much
yellow is involved,
or red.

Which brings me to your heart.
Is it under the beaten quilt of your pain?
Lashed by the ropes of your rage?
Is it in the gap between your insults or burning in the fuel of your jokes?
I felt it once. I know. I think you hate it that I know.

A Lot

I didn't die in the car, I died when you looked aside.
I didn't die under the waves, I died when you watched me crawl up the stairs.
I didn't die in childbirth, I died when you came back with
scratches on your back.
I didn't die in the fires, I died when you hurt the children.
I didn't die under the knife, I died when you watched my blood run.
I didn't die, although I am closer now.
I lied to myself for that time.
I have some life left and a little life, as you know, is a lot of life.

Slam

Are you a door slammer, though?
What door do you slam?
What breaks when you slam that door?
And when you don't have that door, what do you slam?
If you can?
Asking for a friend.

I Didn't See That Coming

There I am, on a boat or as if on a boat, either way,
I was only on a boat like this once, but I remember
—
finally caught the wind, my hair was long and whippy,
my spirits flying along, I'm managing this thing,
tacking well —
and the sail tears.
A great tear in the sail.

That Feeling When.

This will take time.

Rebound

Had a rock. Skipped a rock. Squeezed a rock it didn't bleed.
Threw a rock. Stacked a rock. Buried a rock it didn't seed.
Crept to shelter under a rock, silent so I wouldn't plead.

Rebound.

I am my child's mother. I am my mother's child.
Rock of earth elliptical smile
We're all mama, all the while.

Rebound.

A hundred years a second clock
Back around round rock.

What Was It?

Prompt:
Record an abstract of a conflict you have had, or that you have witnessed.

No
conflict in my life
said the young lady
coming up blank.

The others shared, and her head bowed slightly, as the event took place again inside.

Blueprint
used to be
my favorite word
until I used it
in a sentence
with redline.

healing is a growth stock

I'm Not Done

I thought I was on the bottom step but no.
There was another below that well
I took it down.

Knowing You Then Is Saving Me Now

I was known kindly, once upon.
Any lack of linearity
does not bother me.
I'm ok with it,
because I am.

Every Little Fucking Thing Is a Masterpiece

The great big crow flying easy through
dense branches. My cat padding
toward me after I feed him. The grafted geranium rooting
in new soil. The wind.

You Asked and I Answered

I am the zero and the one
I am the code and the breaker
I am the light and the dark
I am the sucker and the punch
I am the breadth and the length.
I am the yee and the haw
I am the toe and the line.
I am the slaughter and the cow.
I am the x and the y and also the z,
the Q and the A.

La Tina

You know my friend? Her debut as La Tina? The red dress, perfect. She
flows the red dress and owns the ground she spikes in heels. Her lips just
so, in synch. *Quizás, Quizás, Quizás.*

Her legs prepped for bare moments of reveal, moving to the dress,
dancing with their own mind, a revelation.
Her eyelashes sling and rise in a spell casting all of us.
La Tina invites, adores and merges Woman of Uncanny Magic.

The tilt of her head! The focus of her eyes! Level like the hunting animal
with a hip sway. The fan over her shoulder
sends the crowd wild. She suffers
for it, she says, but the effect!
La Tina hits the sweet spot.

The nerve.

I have a red dress. I don't wear it. I have heels and I can dance in them. Not with the red dress, though.

On off, on off, again and again this Mystique the Feminine Routine.

It has historically not ended well. It's relentless.

The difference? La Tina tells me *you have a vagina* using a tone I don't know and I wish I did.

For this diamond slip of time, La Tina brings it all. Star and starlight. Still, it is a risk. She defies the violence I know, so close I can smell it.

Other ladies watch, sparkling with awe and joy. We share this angry joy insurgency.

> The other queens come on and off the stage.
> Vogue in heels like ladder rungs.
> So unsettling, this habit, no matter who does it.
> Relax your ankles when you walk in heels.
> Relax your hips, your knees.
> Know that step one already includes step two.

La Tina, did it take a lifetime to create these moments in the lights? This immeasurable?

Revel in that. I do.

Snap

A length of elasticity seems playful, unruly.
Who knew?
Love would not snap.

A Ripe Mango

A ripe mango, properly cut,
Sweet and drippy,
Throws a cold northern morning.

The Lost Grip II

I lost my grip and fell
from the metal scaffold threat to hang me,
make it my mistake for letting go.

I slipped through the order of chattel grooming,
understood I was not meant to know or
see truth unmarked and non-reflective.

Baited and stamped by colonial imprint like, like?
a factory-farmed animal, a stealth model demanding
I further whiten my knuckles.

I lost my grip on silence, with courage I didn't know I had.
I got it from those who know what free is and what it's not.

Eventually, the sheets reveal what's underneath by the negative space
left around them. The shape becomes distinct.
There have been many victims.

Sky, Open

> *Centuries of cooperation bait our fascination.*
> *Extraordinary architecture,*

drones the teacher in the lecture

My voice rises despite my training the whole sky opens and everything is raining:

> *The constant insurrections are not coincidental!*

Teacher calls me temperamental:

> *I say what's real.*
> *No matter what you feel.*

I hold on to what I know.
They call me wrong, and I say So.

The Fall

Darkness arrives, seems early. The black splash
of night already here, you allude
to the season coming.

I see you.

I devote myself to the dwindling light, counting
what it takes, whatever it takes,
to remember it.

I shelter my candle and see love by its glow.
Our hearts can be our sun and swath the way.

We will look in awe at our plates and cups, our footprints from the bath,
and see the happiness in them, the brightest bit of all,

all of that,
and the sullen cloud beyond which —

Thank You, I'm Sorry

after Jericho Brown's Say Thank You, Say I'm Sorry

Oh child, today's lesson is:

I'm sorry.

I didn't understand your screams were cries for help.

You hoped I would add it up myself but I didn't.
Thank you for helping me, I needed your help.

I'm glad it was only a few years after that day, not decades or a lifetime, that you came to me.

Now I say again that I love you always and now you can believe me.

Compás Beat

The rain, the heat
the compás beat.

Trees close together
sound a clack I
take to mean
and —

ONE
Wind gasp
TWO
Tree clack
THREE.

Step on ONE and THREE
we are dancing with the trees.

Sometimes I Like It Windy

Floating is how it's always been for me.
Bits of me untethered.
Done now, sandbagging myself into your comfort zone,
done resisting pleasure.
Welcome, then,
turbulence.

Stay

The phantom ring tingles on my finger and reminds me
of the married times, and although I want to
shelter there, I find no shelter.

Sometimes
I wear a ring and call it my engagement ring.

In this way I stay engaged.

Or Else, Or ...

Clouds looking all ellipsey, row, plume, row, plume, row, plume.
You see that?
As if the world earth knows you're trying to make me believe otherwise.
My heart leaps to those clouds and the world earth invites me, too.

I turn back toward you and see a guard getting otherwise ready,
pointing at me, setting me aside, not unguarded.

I remember sitting with Rinpoche under the summer clouds
        — this is what they mean by cognitive dissonance —
by the sea, watching the gulls fly, hearing him tell me, six months like this,
and put his wrists together in front, six months like this,
wrists together behind. He had a small window where he saw
clouds and listened to the birds call.

Never left to what I know? Only to your or-else?
I'll name you now, boss. I will name you.
I curl the jail bars open, because the clouds form ellipses.

The Art

When I helped the bird fly — injured by
the cat — nursed back to right —
I did not flap its wings.

Hitch

My heart stopped
— a hiccup —
then beat again
— hitch —
beat the hiccup and hitch,
rhythm with the base line.

Coincidentally

He was standing just outside the door and tipped his head side to side and said *I have one passenger – my head.*

We laughed.

Such a coincidence, I said, *because just this morning, brushing my hair, I said to myself, it's like a passenger.*

My self, I groom and feed and exercise.

We laughed again.

He and his passenger walked away. I went back inside with mine.

Trust

Robins flock in the tree.
Below them, 9 inches of new snow cover the ground.
The earth hugs its warmth and holds their food.
The snow. The snow. But the robins know.

On *The Heart Sutra*

I reeled in my heart on a fishing line
pierced.
The line
stitched
        me
           in
              a
          loop
         to
     the
  fisher.

3 Jewels: A Commentary

A treasure chest this musty metal box
lid opens easily. I undo the rotty cord and look inside.
Fiber packing crumbles at my touch. I gently separate what looks
solid but rises as dust
vapors waft and smell of life and
lives past and present,
Teachings. I am still with the contents of this emptiness,
no relic, no recognizable thing,
nothing there after all,
but my gift.

Lift

The fog lifts, cool pressed
up by
warm earth below meets the sun. I
watch, from a hill, a gap of clarity open,
the not-stuff
not-dirt
not-water.

Touch Me with Your Tactile Heart

Brace for impact. Kiss me to zero sum, then
come unbalance me. Come, we'll drop & roll
away from probability.
Come, we'll dip past ekphrastic, jubilate,
game up higher.

App Quit, Rip

I heard them say *I've been redirected.*
That player's whack. You have point two seconds to click.
You get mana. Wait, what?

A world floats in the interface.
Gravity pulls this user close.
Travel time from wait to what.
Bardo.

Although I have tried to levitate
for years now I can only do it in
twilight moments and there have been no witnesses, or?

Slow — all the animals know.
Birds are all about it. Skunk babies take their turn.
Nightbloomers take it in. Day flowers wrap. Or?

I'm in the city and lights come in fluted texture,
music, setting and illuminating.

My breath in turns and becomes my breath out.

Travel time from wait to what.

Fast — Godspeed, unexpected sneeze.
Glass unbroken, then shards.
My mother alive, then not.

You have a good idea.

Notes:

The poem "Escaping the Gaze" uses material from the Wikipedia article Mirror (https://en.wikipedia.org/wiki/Mirror) which is released under the Creative Commons Attribution-ShareAlike 3.0 license.

The poem "Disappeared / Desaparecido" is an ode for the estimated 30,000 people who, thought to be politically or ideologically even a vague threat, disappeared during the United States-backed military junta in Argentina from 1976 to 1983. They were killed in an attempt by the junta to silence the social and political opposition.

The poem "On *The Heart Sutra*" references the fundamental Buddhist text that states, "Form is emptiness. Emptiness is form. Emptiness is not other than form. Form is not other than emptiness."

In the poem "La Tina," *Quizás, Quízas, Quizás* is a Spanish language song attributed to Trío Los Panchos.

Also Available from Rootstock Publishing:

The Atomic Bomb on My Back
Taniguchi Sumiteru

Blue Desert
Celia Jeffries

China in Another Time: A Personal Story
Claire Malcolm Lintilhac

Fly with A Murder of Crows: A Memoir
Tuvia Feldman

Junkyard at No Town
J.C. Myers

The Inland Sea
Sam Clark

The Language of Liberty:
A Citizen's Vocabulary
Edwin C. Hagenstein

Lucy Dancer
Story and Illustrations
by Eva Zimet

Nobody Hitchhikes Anymore
Ed Griffin-Nolan

Preaching Happiness: Creating a Just
and Joyful World
Ginny Sassaman

Red Scare in the Green Mountains:
Vermont in the McCarthy Era
1946-1960
Rick Winston

Safe as Lightning: Poems
Scudder H. Parker

Street of Storytellers
Doug Wilhelm

Tales of Bialystok: A Jewish Journey from Czarist Russia to America
Charles Zachariah Goldberg

To the Man in the Red Suit: Poems
Christina Fulton

Uncivil Liberties: A Novel
Bernie Lambek

The Violin Family
Melissa Perley; Illustrated by
Fiona Lee Maclean

Wave of the Day: Collected Poems
Mary Elizabeth Winn

Whole Worlds Could Pass Away: Collected Stories
Rickey Gard Diamond

www.ingramcontent.com/pod-product-compliance
Lightning Source LLC
Chambersburg PA
CBHW081431070526
44586CB00020B/2554